Beverage Equipment

Quick Trouble Shooting Guide

CM. Welch

Copyright © 2024 by CM. Welch All rights reserved.

It is not legal to reproduce, duplicate, or transmit any part of this document in either electronic means or in printed format. Recording of this publication is strictly prohibited and any storage of this document is not allowed unless with written permission from the publisher except for the use of brief quotations in a book review.

All rights reserved. Protected under the United States Copyright law.

This book or any portion thereof may not be reproduced or used in any manner whatsoever without the express written permission of the publisher except for the use of brief quotations in a book review.

Cover Design by Define by Lulu

Printed in the United States.

First edition, 2024.

Contents

Introduction   1

1. Preferred Tool List   2

2. Water Filters   5
   Cuno SW3, Cuno SW3-Plus, Everpure CB20-312, Everpure MC Cartridge series
   Changing Water Filters
   TAP 442 ONLY

3. Water Boosters   12
   McCann's 4.4 gallon Multiplex WBK, 8, 9, 10 Water Boosters
   Water booster Pressures for units

4. CO2 Regulators   17
   CO2 Regulators

5. BIB Pumps (Bag in a Box Syrup)   21
   Flojet N 5100 or T 5000, Flojet G55 or G57, Shurflo syrup BIB pump

6. Carbonator   26
   Lancer Turbo High Capacity, McCann's large Reserve (BigMac), Taprite
   Taprite/Schroeder electronic probe quick troubleshooting guide
   Schroeder/Taprite/McCann's

7. Valves   35
   Cornelius UF-1 or SFV-1, Lancer LEV 3.0 or 4.5, Flomatic 424,454,464 Valves

8. Ice Combos   42
   Cornelius ED 150-200-250-300 and DF 150-200-250 units, Cornelius IDC Pro, Cornelius Flavor fusion, Lancer 4500, and IBD 22,30 units, Lancer FLavorSelect, Servend/Multiplex MD150-200 units, Cornelius IDC255 Pro Fast Gate
   Lancer Flavor select and Cornelius Flavor Fusion
   Cornelius IDC Pro

9. Drop In Units   56
   Cornelius CB2323, 1522, 3032, Intellicarb units. Lancer 1523, 2300, 2400 units

10. Bevariety   61

11. Electric Countertop Fountain Machines   65
    Electric countertop Cornelius Olympus and Lancer 1500 - 2500 units

12. Barguns   70

13. Automated beverage system   76
    ABS 1.O
    ABS 1.0 Errors
    ABS 2.0
    Errors

14. Multiplex Chiller   98
    Error Codes

15. Juice Dispenser   107
    Lancer MMJ 2 and MMJ 4 Units

16. Vending Machine   112
    Crane Merchandising systems (Dixie Narco)
    Dixie DN 3800 - DN 5800
    Royal 550, 600, 670, 804 machines
    RVV 500 Vision Vendor (Royal glass front machine)
    Vendo V21 series Vmax 521-V621-V721-V821 Vending machines

References   140

Introduction

As a Beverage System Technician with nearly 20 years of experience under my belt, I've seen just about everything that can go wrong with beverage dispensers. From the simple hiccups to the head-scratching mysteries, I've faced them all. Over the years, I've learned that sometimes, the best solutions come from the field, not from a manual.

That's why I decided to put together this trouble shooting guide. I've crafted it with one goal in mind: to make your job easier. I know firsthand how frustrating it can be to sort through technical jargon or follow lengthy procedures when all you want is to get the system back up and running. This guide is filled with shortcuts, tips, and practical advice I've picked up over the years. It's designed to help you diagnose and fix problems quickly, so you can get back to what you do best—ensuring customers enjoy a perfect beverage, every time.

Whether you're a seasoned technician or just starting out, I hope this guide becomes your go-to resource in the field. Let's dive in and start solving problems together.

Chapter 1

Preferred Tool List

This is a suggested tool list that I and many other techs have needed to work on most equipment you will see in the field.

This is the minimum needed, and some people like using different tools to make jobs easier. But this is what I carried in my tool bag every day to get the job done. If you want to carry 100 pounds of specialty tools, feel free to do so. But as you will soon realize, a light tool bag is easier to tote around. Keep the specialty tools in the truck and use them when needed.

- 5 in 1 screwdriver and or #1 and #2 Phillips and Flathead screwdrivers

- Nut driver set ¼, 5/16, ⅜, 7/16 minimum

- Needle nose locking vice grips x2

PREFERRED TOOL LIST

- Utility knife
- Wrenches ⅜, 7/16, ½, 9/16, ¾ combination wrenches set
- Allen wrench set
- Digital tire pressure gauge
- Needle-nose pliers
- Dykes (side cutter diagonal wire cutting pliers)
- 9" or "10 Phillips and flathead screwdriver
- 10" crescent wrench (adjustable wrench)
- 9.5" channel locks (tongue-and-groove pliers)
- 9" ear clamp pliers front and side jaw (Oetiker clamp pliers)
- Hose and tubing cutter (for cutting beverage line)
- Flashlight
- Wire strippers
- Socket set up to 3/4 " ⅜ drive, and ¼" drive 9mm or 11/32 deep well socket
- 25" Tape measure
- AC voltage tester (AC sensor pen)

- Digital thermometer (probe type)

- Cordless drill

- Ratio/Brix cup and syrup separators for valves working on

- Bar Gun O-ring insert and removal tool

- Flow control extractor tool for lancer valves

- Multimeter

- True door spring tension tool x2

Chapter 2

Water Filters

Water filters are used to remove unwanted impurities from water. They help ensure a better tasting product by removing things like sediment and bacteria to increase water quality.

Cuno SW3, Cuno SW3-Plus, Everpure CB20-312, Everpure MC Cartridge series

Most water filter systems have an incoming and outgoing water pressure gauge.

If not, reading pressure on the incoming side:

- ensure if possible to have at least 45 psi water pressure supplying filters.

- ensure all water shut offs are in the open position.

- possible defective pressure gauge (pressure gauge needle sticking).

If the outgoing pressure is not reading, or the pressure is dropping then climbing back up:

- Change water filters

- Possible defective pressure gauge

Outgoing water pressure should always maintain a minimum of 25 PSI. If it drops below 25 PSI or goes to zero, it will introduce air into the system causing flat drinks and can also cause premature failure of the water booster or carbonator pump.

Changing Water Filters

Step 1 – Disconnect power to all water booster and carbonator motors.

Step 2 – Shut off water supply to filters.

Step 3 – In a drain or bucket, open purge or flush valve to depressurize the system (gauge reading zero). If no valve is available, run the plain water valve on equipment till water stops flowing.

Step 4 – Change water filters (follow Filters Housing recommendations for cleaning filter housings).

Step 5 – Turn water supply back on.

Step 6 – In drain or bucket, open purge flush valve and run it till you get a clear steam to ensure all air and debris is out of the system (minimum of 5 gallons normally).

Step 7 – Connect power to the water booster first, if equipped, then carbonators. Cycle carbonators two – three times to ensure proper flow.

Step 8 – Done :) Ready to serve.

Antunes water filter system VZN 441-V and Tap442

No power:

- Unit unplugged or no power on outlet.

- Check for broken wires.

- Possible defective controller or incorrect power to controller.

System not flushing or continuously flushing.

- Possible foreign debris in flush solenoid or defective solenoid. Replace solenoid.

Low water flow:

- In coming water from the water booster is too low.

- Possible outlet valve clogged or defective.

Low or no water from filter system.

- Possible clogged filters.

- Check for a defective bladder in the tank and ensure proper PSI. PSI must be checked when tank is empty (no water in tank).

- Check to ensure the rinse ball valve is completely in the off position.

- Check to ensure the inlet and outlet valves are in the full open position.

TAP 442 ONLY

Water not filling ultra filter:

- Possible defective inlet solenoid.

- No power to the controller.

Water not flowing from ultra filter:

- Possible defective permeate solenoid.

- No power to controller.

Controller says flow rate error:

- Possible defective flow meter.

System flushing at time of high water use:

- Ensure that the controller clock and flush time are set correctly.

NOTES

NOTES

Chapter 3
Water Boosters

Water boosters boost water pressure, ensuring consistent water pressure to the carbonators and beverage equipment.

McCann's 4.4 gallon Multiplex WBK, 8, 9, 10 Water Boosters

Water booster continuously running But Not Building pressure:

- Verify sufficient water supply.

- Insufficient water supply to the Booster pump. Check the water shut-off valve isn't in the off position.

- Possible water filters clogged.

- Possible bad water booster pump (brass pump).

- Possible defective check valve not allowing water to pass through or causing back pressure.

Water Booster continuously cycles on and off rapidly between the cut in and cut off pressure settings:

- Normally caused by Ruptured Bladder in the tank. Verify by air fitting on the booster tank by pressing in the Schrader valve. If water comes out. Replace the tank.

- Ensure proper air PSI charge on tank (must be checked with no water in tank).

Water booster not turning on but making humming noise:

Possible bad booster pump or motor.

- Separate pump from motor and connect power to booster. If the motor turns on and starts spinning, replace pump (brass pump). If motor hums and does not spin, replace the motor.

Water booster Pressures for units

Most legacy equipment - cut in at 60 psi - cut off at 80 psi.

- Installed after water filters.

Multiplex cut in at 70 psi - cut out at 90 psi.

- Normally installed after pre filter and before main filters.

Freestyle cut in at 80 psi - cute out at 100 psi.

- Installed before water filters.

NOTES

NOTES

Chapter 4

CO2 Regulators

A CO2 Regulator is used to control the pressure from a compressed gas tank to ensure the supply correct pressures needed for BIB pumps and carbonators.

CO2 Regulators

High pressure regulator setting per unit:

- External carbonators (non-cold carb units) Cornelius, Mc-

Cann's, Lancer, Taprite – 105 PSI.

- Most cold carb units (built-in carb tank) – 75 PSI.

- ABS 1.0 and 2.0 – 90 PSI.

- Freestyle (7000-7100-8000) – 70 PSI. (9000) 80 – PSI. (8100 - 9100) – 75 PSI.

BIB operating pressures for fountain units:

- **Standard Ice combo** – 65 PSI.

- **Standard Drop in unit** – 65 PSI.

- **Bevariety** – 75 PSI.

- **Freestyle** (8000 and 9000) – 80 PSI. (7000-7100-8100-9100) – 70 PSI.

CO2 leak at tank connection:

- Defective worn quad ring or seal.

- Possible hairline crack on regulator.

- Issue with CO2 tank.

CO2 leak on regulator housing:

- CO2 Leaking from the weep hole is caused by a defective diaphragm in the regulator. Replace diaphragm or regulator.

CO2 leaking from safety relief valve (on back of regulator):

- Possible overfilled CO2 tank (full tank is normally between 800-1000 PSI full).

- **Defective diaphragm** — You will see the outgoing pressure needle running away. It's caused from unregulated CO2 pressure causing the safety valve to release. Replace diaphragm or regulator.

Unable to adjust CO2 pressure:

- CO2 low or empty tank.

- Tank valve not in the on or open position.

- Possible broken diaphragm adjustment spring.

- Possible stuck pressure reading needle on gauge.

- If it has a plastic adjustment handle, it could possibly be stripped.

- If the tank is frozen, it will lower the tank pressure and will not allow it to adjust properly.

NOTES

Chapter 5

BIB Pumps (Bag in a Box Syrup)

BIB pumps deliver syrup from the bag-in-a-box syrup to the beverage dispensing equipment using CO2 or compressed air.

Flojet N 5100 or T 5000, Flojet G55 or G57, Shurflo syrup BIB pump

Not pumping – no syrup to unit:

- No air or CO_2 to pump.

- BIB connector not screwed on properly.

- Kink in BIB suction line (clear Tygon tubing).

- If pre chiller, multiplex, or electric countertop, check for frozen with bath.

- CO_2 line not engaged when put into pump means possible bent or broke quick release pin or possible broke or cracked pin engager in the bottom of the pump.

- Defective BIB pump.

Pump continuously pumping:

- Check for hole in BIB bag.

- BIB tubing kinked.

- Empty BIB box or BIB connector not screwed on all the way.

- Possible worn or defective BIB connector.

- With new BIB changed, you may need to purge air from system by running the dispenser valve.

- Defective BIB pump.

CO2 leaking at pump:

- Cracked or damaged CO2 supply fitting.

- Missing or damaged CO2 supply fitting O-ring.

- Leak on the pump itself or bad diaphragm (replace pump).

Water in CO2 line or coming out of exhaust port on BIB pump:

- Bad CO2 supply line check valve (backflow preventer) on carbonator tank.

BIB bag blowing up (inflating):

- Replace BIB changeover valve (bag selector).

BIB vent:

- Helps to reduce air in the system, which causes excess foam in drinks.

BIB operating pressures for fountain units:

- **Standard Ice combo** – 65 PSI.

- **Standard Drop in unit** – 65 PSI.

- **Bevariety** – 75 PSI.

- **Freestyle** (8000 and 9000) – 80 PSI.

(7000-7100-8100-9100) – 70 PSI.

High pressure regulator settings:

- **External carb** (non cold carb units): Cornelius, McCann's, Lancer, Taprite – 105 PSI.

- **Most cold carb units** (built in carb tank) – 75 PSI.

- **ABS** 1.0 and 2.0 to carb tank – 90 PSI.

- **Freestyle** (7000-7100-8000) – 70 PSI. (9000) – 80 PSI. (8100-9100) – 75 PSI.

Flojet G55 or G57 BIBpumps	Flojet T5000 or N5100 BIB pumps	Shurflo BIB pump
5 GPM Flow rate 100 PSI Max Pressure Liquid Temp Range 40 degrees to 120 degrees Fahrenheit	2.5 GPM flow rate 80 psi max pressure Liquid temp range 40 degree 120 degrees Fahrenheit	85 psi max pressure Liquid temp range 34 degree 120 degrees Fahrenheit

NOTES

Chapter 6

Carbonator

The carbonators job is to deliver carbonated water to the beverage dispenser by infusing carbon dioxide gas (CO2) into water thus making soda water.

Lancer Turbo High Capacity, McCann's large Reserve (BigMac), Taprite

- Lancer turbo – High capacity – Cornelius large reserve low profile – Most cold carb units.

Carbonator not turning on (blowing air from valves):

- Verify correct power source - no power.

- Possible defective liquid level control board or probe. Verify by disconnecting green probe wire from the board. If it turns on and runs, replace probe. If does not run, possible defective board.

- Possible carb time out due to insufficient water supply. Reset the carbonator.

Carbonator or not turning on but making humming noise:

- Possible defective carb pump or motor. Separate the pump from the motor and turn on the power to the carbonator. If the motor turns on and starts spinning, replace the pump (brass pump). If the motor hums and does not spin, replace the motor.

Carbonator runs continuously and times out:

- Verify sufficient water supply.

- Possible bad carb pump (brass pump).

If continues to run and blows relief valve on carb tank:

- Possible defective liquid level control board or probe. Verify by creating a 3-wire jumper, all three wires tied together at one end, and three spade connectors on the other end. Remove the probe wires from the board (Hi-Lo-G) and connect the 3-wire jumper to Hi-Lo-G. Turn power back on. If it continues to run, replace the board. If it does not run, replace the probe.

Drinks dispense with low carbonation (flat drinks):

- CO_2 low or empty. Verify correct CO_2 pressure for unit (see regulator section).

- Possible high water pressure exceeding CO_2 pressure (may need an in line water pressure regulator).

- Ensure ice is in the ice bin covering the cold-plate and drinks are below 41 degrees F.

- Possible defective atomizer in carb tank causing low dispersion of CO_2 into water, replace tank (less common).

- Air entering system due to low water pressure – possible clogged water filters.

- Possible collapsed soda water beverage line (less common).

Taprite/Schroeder electronic probe quick troubleshooting guide

Green light illuminated is normal operation. If green light is on and is not running – possible faulty probe control module.

Red light illuminated is normally due to long run time.

- Possible defective carb pump or motor.

- Defective probe control module.

No light on module:

- Verify correct power and wiring on motor. If correct, replace probe control module.

Schroeder/Taprite/McCann's

Carb not turning on (blowing air from valves):

- Verify correct power on outlet, also ensure carb power cord is plugged in to wall outlet and probe connection on carb is plugged in properly.

- Possible defective carb probe - switch or float.

- If the carbonator is hot or making a humming noise there is a possible defective carb pump (brass pump) or motor. Verify by separating the pump from the motor. Connect power to the carbonator. If the motor hums and does not spin, replace the motor. If the motor starts spinning, replace the carbonator pump.

Carbonator runs continuously:

- Verify correct water pressure is supplying carbonator pump (min 25 PSI).

- Possible defective carb pump.

- Possible weak or defective carb motor not spinning pump.

- Possible leaking soda water line causing pump to never satisfy carb.

- Defective backflow preventer.

Carb runs continuously and blows relief valve on carb tank:

- Defective carb probe – replace switch or float.

Backflow preventer leaking:

- Replace the backflow preventer.

Water leaking from weep hole on carb pump:

- Replace the carbonator pump (brass pump).

Drinks dispense with low carbonation (flat drinks):

- Verify correct CO_2 pressure for the unit (see regulator section).

- Possible high water pressure exceeding CO_2 pressure (may need water regulator to reduce pressure to 50 PSI).

- Ensure ice is in ice bin covering cold-plate and drinks below 41 degrees F.

- Air entering water system due to low water pressure – possibly clogged water filters.

- Possible defective atomizer in carb tank causing low dispersion of CO_2 into water – replace carb tank.

- Possible collapsed line from the carbonator to fountain unit.

- Customer cups not properly rinsed, leaving soap residue on the cups affecting carbonation. Verify by using foam or plastic cup to taste test.

CO_2 backing up into water system:

- Defective check valve (backflow preventer). Plain water valve will sometimes dispense carb water.

Water in CO_2 lines going to pumps:

- Defective CO_2 check valve on carb tank.

Water leaking from fittings:

- Possible defective nylon flare washer.

Start up procedure or restoring carbonated water (normally possible to start with Step 3):

Step 1 – Disconnect power to carb.

Step 2 – Shut CO_2 off and water on. Open the relief valve on the carb tank till water starts to come out close to the relief valve (normally can skip this step and proceed to step 3).

Step 3 — Shut water off and turn CO2 on run fountain equipment till water is out of system and air is dispensing from equipment (gassing out).

Step 4 — Turn the water supply back on and connect power to the carbonator. Wait till it carbonator cycles on and turns off.

Step 5 — Dispense fountain equipment to purge all air from lines till a steady flow of soda water is dispensed (ensure not to outrun carbonator fill time by dispensing too many valves at once).

NOTES

NOTES

Chapter 7

Valves

Valves are utilized to maintain a consistent and high-quality beverage by accurately dispensing the proper mixture (ratio) of product and water or soda water.

Cornelius UF-1 or SFV-1, Lancer LEV 3.0 or 4.5, Flomatic 424, 454, 464 Valves

Flat drinks or off taste:

- Low CO2 pressure (see carbonator section for more info).

- No ice in ice bin or on cold-plate.

- Check for proper ratio.

- Carbonator issue (see carb section).

Foamy drinks:

- There is no ice in the ice bin or on the cold-plate (dispensed product must be below 41 degrees F).

- Air in syrup BIB lines, check for hole in BIB bag, loose or defective BIB connector.

- Possible defective O-ring or fitting on suction side or BIB pump.

- High soda water flow.

- Loose, missing, dirty, or defective nozzle or diffuser.

- Possibly need to add BIB vent.

Valve dispenses air and syrup only:

- No water from the carbonator (see carbonator section).

Valve dispenses water but no syrup:

- If it is an electric countertop or has a pre-chiller, ensure the water bath is not frozen.

- Empty BIB, kinked BIB line, or no CO2 to BIB pump (see BIB section for more info).

- Obstructed flow control or broken flow control spring.

- Swollen or broken paddle arm.

- Shut off on the back block is in the off position.

- **UF-1 or SFV-1 valve** – ensure the back block is in the full open position (pushed up and release lever at bottom snapped into place).

- **UF-1 or SFV-1 valve** – possible defective back block. **Flomatic valve** – possible broken coil spring paddle arm retainer.

Valve dispense syrup but no carb water:

- Shut-off valve on the carb water line is in the off position.

- Possible carb issues (see carb section).

- Obstructed flow control or broken flow control spring.

- Swollen or broken paddle arm.

- If pre-chiller, electric countertop, or multiplex, check to ensure water bath is not frozen.

- Ensure the back block shut-off is in the 'on' position.

- **UF-I or SFV-I** — ensure the back block is in the full 'open' position (push up and release lever snapped into place lock position).

- Possible broken coil spring paddle arm retainer **Flomatic valves.**

Low soda or low syrup flow:

- Foreign debris in the flow controls.

- Worn yoke, bad armature, or defective solenoid.

- Swollen paddle arms.

- Improper ratio.

- Kinked or collapsed water syrup lines.

- If electric countertop, pre-chiller, or multiplex, check for frozen water bath. **UF-1 or SFV-1** — ensure the back block is in the full 'open' position (push up and release lever until snapped into place. This is the lock position).

Non carb valve dispensing carb water:

- Replace the check valve (backflow preventer on carbonator tank).

Valve not activating or sputtering:

- No power to unit.

- Key switch not on or is a defective key switch.

- Corroded or broken wires from transformer to key switch.

- Valve wiring loose or corroded on solenoid connections.

- Defective valve lever switch.

- **UF-I or SFV-1** – bottom plate not snapped into place properly, not allowing lever to engage switch.

- Possible defective transformer or tripped breaker on the transformer. If tripped or continuously tripping the breaker on the transformer, it's possible a bare wire is grounding out on the unit or there is a weak transformer. Most common problem if the transformer is tripping is that a wire is pinched on the back block or around the sliding ice bin lid.

- Broken or missing lever or lever electric retainer **Flomatic valves.**

Water leaking water or syrup leaking from valve:

- Pin hole in valve body – replace.

- Pin hole in back block or back block O-rings bad.

- Possible crack on lower valve body.

- Paddle arms not seated properly.

- Foreign debris on the paddle arms not allowing them to seat properly.

- Flow control body O-rings defective valve system quad seal on back block **UF-1 or SFV-1.**

- Pin hole in flow control body **UF-1 or SFV-1.**

Valve sticking and running continuously:

- Sticky lever or valve switch.

- Defective solenoid or armature.

- Worn or broken yoke. **LEV valves.**

Valve not adjusting or won't ratio:

- Ensure BIB is not empty, the BIB line is not kinked, and the BIB connector is screwed on properly.

- Possible debris in flow control or broken spring.

- Ensure proper size flow control (syrup and water flow control not crossed).

- Possible swollen paddle arms (banjo).

NOTES

Chapter 8

Ice Combos

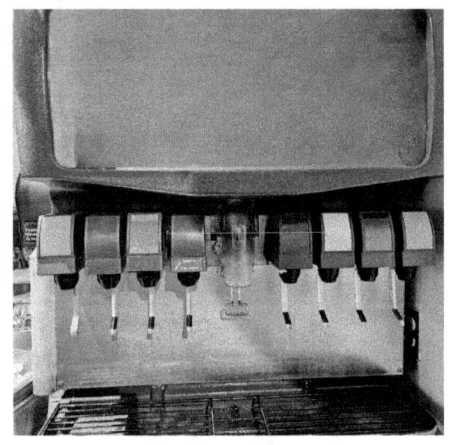

Ice combo beverage fountain machines are normally found in self-serve applications consisting of 6 to 16 valve fountain machines with a push lever activated ice dispenser for customer use. Uses ice to ensure the product is dispensed at the proper temperature.

Cornelius ED 150-200-250-300 and DF 150-200-250 units, Cornelius IDC Pro, Cornelius Flavor fusion, Lancer 4500, and IBD 22,30 units, Lancer FLavorSelect, Servend/Multiplex MD150-200 units, Cornelius IDC255 Pro Fast Gate

ALL ICE COMBOS

Ice dispense randomly:

- Ice slipping through the ice gate due to play in the gate. Loosen screws on the ice gate solenoid and lower solenoid till black ice gate rests against the opening. Takes free play out of the ice gate **(Lancer only)**.

- Jammed or broken ice gate or solenoid.

- No CO2 to ice gate cylinder causing it to stay in the open position **(IDC255 Fast Gate only)**.

- Jammed or defective ice gate cylinder **(IDC255 Fast Gate only)**.

Ice dispensing continuously:

- Ice chute spring missing or broken **(Lancer only)**.

- Defective ice dispense switch.

- Broken lower or upper ice chute.

Ice not dispensing (all units):

- Ice bin empty.
- Defective ice dispenser switch.
- Broken or loose wire on ice dispenser switch.
- Weak or defective ice gate solenoid.
- Ice frozen together or chunks of ice blocking the ice chute.
- Defective ice agitator motor.
- Broken or damaged ice agitator blade or wheel.

Not dispensing ice Cornelius (IDC255 Pro Fast Gate only):

- The ice bin is empty.
- If the ice gate is not opening, ensure the main CO_2 supply is on and supplying the ice gate cylinder (controlled by ice gate solenoid preset at 35 PSI)
- Possible defective ice gate cylinder.
- Clumps of ice blocking the ice gate opening.
- Ensure the ice chute cover is properly attached and not missing a magnet.
- Possible defective ice agitator motor not spinning allowing ice to fill ice chute.

- Possible faulty ice chute magnetic switch.

- Possible broken agitator blade or wheel.

- If portion controls are not working, ensure the automatic/manual switch is in the automatic position and the power switch is on. If the green light between the power and automatic switch is on, the machine is in manual mode and the ice portion controls will not work.

Water leak from back of ice chute:

- Check for cracked upper ice chute or damaged foam or plastic where ice chute mounts to unit.

- Possible defective ice chute gasket **(Cornelius only)**.

Ice motor runs but ice is not dispensing:

- Pin or clip not attached or missing that connects ice gate solenoid to ice gate.

- Defective ice gate solenoid to ice gate.

- Defective board.

Ice gate opens but motor does not active or dispense ice:

- Check if the ice is frozen together in the ice bin.

- Possible defective ice agitator motor or harness not connected.

Adjusting ice dispense flow:

- Loosen screws on ice gate solenoid and slide up to increase flow and slide down to decrease flow.

- Loosen nuts holding ice chute to unit and slide restrictor plate up to increase flow and down to decrease flow **(Cornelius only)**.

Blowing fuse or tripping breaker:

- Possible short in wiring.

- Defective ice agitator motor.

- Defective ice gate solenoid.

Valves not activating or no power:

- Transformer or power supply not plugged into outlet. Ensure the breaker is not tripped on transformer.

- Breaker or loose wires from transformer to key switch.

- Key switch not in the on position or defective key switch.

- Possible faulty transformer.

- Possible valves issues (see valves sections).

Lancer Flavor select and Cornelius Flavor Fusion

Not dispensing drinks when button pressed:

- Possible defective touch pad switch assembly.
- Ensure breakers on the machine are not tripped.
- Check all valve harnesses are connected properly.

Soda water or Plain water not dispensing:

- Ensure water and CO_2 pressures are correct.
- Check the soda valve is on the back block correctly and that the line coming from the solenoid is not pinched.
- Remove flow control and check for foreign debris or a broken spring.
- Check solenoid plunger for a swollen tip.
- Possible defective solenoid.
- Possible loose connection on valve wire harness.
- Possible defective board.
- See carb section for more info.

Not dispensing syrup:

- Check for empty BIB.

- Ensure BIB connector is screwed on properly.

- Make sure the BIB line is not kinked.

- CO2 is on and connected to the BIB pump.

- Ensure the valve is secured/seated on the back block correctly and in the on position and line from solenoid is not pinched.

- Remove flow control and check for foreign debris and that the spring is not broken.

- Check solenoid plunger for a swollen tip.

- Possible weak or defective solenoid.

- Possible loose connection on valve wire harness.

- Possible defective board.

See Lancer or Cornelius ice combo section for more troubleshooting.

Cornelius IDC Pro

75 PSI CO2 to carbonator deck

65 PSI CO2 to BIB pumps

50-65 PSI water regulator

12 VDC powers MFV board

30 VDC power to solenoids

Soda water is not dispensing or plain water:

- Ensure there are no breakers tripped.

- Ensure correct water and Co_2 pressures.

- Check to ensure the valve is on the back block correctly and that the shut-off is in the open position.

- Remove the flow control and check for foreign debris or a broken spring.

- Check that the solenoid plunger tip is not swollen or that the solenoid plunger housing is rusty.

- Possible weak solenoid not pulling up plunger.

- If you've replaced the solenoid assembly, and it's still not activating, there is possibly a faulty wire harness, wire connection, or detective MFV board.

- If you find yourself replacing the same solenoid over the course of a few weeks or months, suspect a defective wire harness to the solenoids.

- Co_2 pressure is too high.

- If blowing air from valves, see carbonator section for more info.

NOT dispensing syrup:

- Ensure the breakers are not tripped.

- Check for empty BIB.

- BIB connector is screwed on properly and BIB line is not kinked.

- CO_2 supply is on and set to 65 PSI and connected to bottom of the BIB pump.

- Make sure the shut-off on the back block is in the 'on' position.

- Remove the flow control and check for foreign debris or broken spring.

- Remove the syrup solenoid and check for a swollen plunger tip or rusty plunger housing.

- Possible weak solenoid not pulling up plunger.

- If you replaced the solenoid and it's still not activating, suspect a faulty wire harness or wire connections check for 30VDC.

- Possible defective MFV board.

NOT dispensing ice:

- The ice bin is empty.

- Clumps of ice could be blocking the ice gate opening.

- Touch screen is not closed properly, engaging the switch.

- Ice chute not installed properly or broken.

- Possible defective ice chute switch (sensor).

- Ensure the breaker is not tripped.

- If it has an ice fill lid, ensure lid is secure to unit properly/installed. Also check for missing magnet for sensor.

- Possible faulty sensor harness from agitator board.

- Possible defective agitation board.

- Check to ensure the ice is not frozen together in ice bin.

- Possible defective ice agitator motor.

- Check for broken or damaged agitator blade or wheel.

Ice dispensing continuously or randomly:

- Ensure the ice gate is not stuck in the 'open' position and moving freely.

- Ensure the ice chute assembly is installed properly.

Flat or off taste drinks:

- Check for proper CO_2 pressure (75 PSI to carbonator)

- Ensure there is ice in the ice bin and on the cold-plate.

- Improper ratio on valves.

- Missing or dirty diffuser or nozzle assembly.

- Ensure proper water pressure (below 65 PSI).

- If CO_2 just changed, you may need to cycle the carbonator (run 4 to 5 pitchers of soda water or until you get a nice flow of soda water)

- Possible ice bin cold-plate drain line clogged.

- Possible ice has bridged up on cold-plate, not allowing the lines to cool properly.

Water leaking from underneath fountain:

- Check for obstructed cold-plate drain lines.

- Water leaking from the valve or back block.

- Water leaking from the ice chute where it meets the unit.

- Possible leak from the carbonator tank.

Tripping breakers:

- Possible short in the wiring.

- Possible defective ice agitator motor, sensor, board, or solenoid, depending on which breaker is tripping.

Water in ice bin:

- Cold-plate drain lines are clogged.

Entering dashboard screen (menu):

- Start from top right of screen, press top right corner, top left corner, bottom left corner (above drink icon), right bottom corner. 1,2,3,4.

- Menu is used for cleaning procedures, changing to a different brand or flavor, calibrating touch screen, updating software, etc.

Screen image not sized properly and very dim:

- Must resize image (call Cornelius for walk through).

NOTES

NOTES

Chapter 9

Drop In Units

Drop In fountain machines are normally found in crew-serve applications. Drop-in units have an ice well that employees use to scoop ice for drinks. Usually found sitting in a countertop or in a drop-in stand with legs. 6 to 8 valves are the most common. Unit uses ice and a cold-plate to ensure the product is dispensed at the proper temperature.

Cornelius CB2323, 1522, 3032, Intellicarb units. Lancer 1523, 2300, 2400 units

Valves not activating or no power:

- Check for power on the main outlet.

- Transformer or power supply is not plugged into an outlet.

- Ensure the breaker is not tripped on the transformer.

- Check for damaged or loose wires from the transformer to the key switch.

- Key switch is not in the on position or there is a defective key switch.

- Ensure the ice lid switch is connected and the lid is closed.

- Ensure the lid switch is operating properly. If the lid switch is bypassed, ensure the wires are tied together.

- Possible faulty transformer.

- Possible short in the wiring normally found where the back block meets the unit, or the ice lid switch wires are hitting the lid when sliding back.

Flat or foamy drinks (off taste):

- Low to no CO_2 (see carbonator section).

- No ice in the ice bin, chilling the cold-plate.

- Ice bin drain line is clogged and holding water.

- Improper ratio on valves (see valve section).

- Possible ice bridged up on the cold-plate not allowing the lines to cool properly (below 41 degrees F).

- Missing or defective nozzle or diffuser.

Water leaking from fountain:

- Possible valve or back block leaking (see valve section for more info).

- Drain pan is not lined up properly.

- Missing or incorrectly installed drain pan boot.

- Possible clogged drain lines.

Valves blowing air:

- See carbonator section.

Valve problems:

- See valve section.

Not dispensing syrup:

- See BIB section.

- See valve section.

Not dispensing water or soda water:

- See valve section.

- See carbonator section.

NOTES

Chapter 10

Bevariety

MVU valves

MVU valves are multi-flavor valves found on ice combo and drop-in units. Usually found with 3 to 6 flavors on each valve with some having shot capabilities.

Ice combo – see ice combo sector for more troubleshooting

Drop-in unit – see drop in unit section for more troubling shooting

Touchpad not working:

- Verify there is 24 VAC from the transformer to the MVU board. It normally will have lights on the MVU board. If there is no 24 VAC, check power on the outlet to ensure there is 120v to the transformer. If the power is present, ensure the breaker is not tripped on the transformer. If it's not tripped and 24v is not present, replace the transformer. If 24v are present and the MVU board is not lit up, then replace the MVU board. If MVU lights up and the touch pad is responsive, check for faulty, loose, or corroded wire harness from the MVU board to touch pad. If the harness is good, suspect a defective touchpad. If there are multiple touchpads on the unit, you can verify by moving a touch pad temporarily to see if the touchpad fixes the problem.

NOT dispensing syrup:

- See BIB section.

- Possible swollen solenoid plunger tip.

- Possible defective solenoid.

- Faulty or loose wire harness to solenoids.

- Possible defective MVU board.

NOT dispensing water or soda water:

- Possible swollen solenoid plunger tip.

- Possible defective solenoid.

- Loose or defective wire harness to solenoids.

- Possible faulty MVU board.

- See carbonator section for more info.

NOT dispensing ice:

- See ice combo section.

Ice dispenses randomly:

- See ice combo section.

Flat or foamy drinks (off taste):

- See ice combo or drop in unit section.

NOTES

Chapter 11

Electric Countertop Fountain Machines

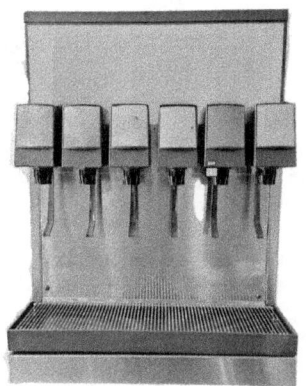

An electric countertop is normally a 6 to 8 valve fountain machine with a built-in pre-chiller to provide ready to drink products without the use of ice and cold-plate. This unit has no ice bin. Customers must have a separate ice bin for ice.

Electric countertop Cornelius Olympus and Lancer 1500 - 2500 units

Water bath frozen:

- Ensure the water bath agitator is spinning and agitating water.

- Possible defective ice bank control not allowing compressor to shut-off.

- Possible detective ice bank control probe or sensor probe not secured in place.

Compressor deck not turning on and running:

- Possible defective ice bank control.

- Defective ice bank control probe.

- Possible TDS level of water below 100 PPM not allowing electrical conductivity through the water. If suspected, drain the water bath and refill with fresh water.

- Possible compressor or compressor component issues.

Valves not activating or no power:

- Check for power on the outlet.

- Transformer or power on the outlet.

- Transformer or power supply not plugged into the outlet and ensure the breaker is not tripped on the transformer.

- Ensure the power and key switch are in the on position.

- Broken or loose wire from transformer to valves.

- Possible issue with the valves (see valve section).

Uneven ice bank:

- Normally caused by low freon or restriction in refrigeration system.

- Ensure the condenser is clean and nothing is restricting air flow to the unit.

- Ice bank control sensor is not in the proper position.

Flat drinks or foamy drinks:

- No ice bank chilling drinks to the proper temp of 41 degrees F.

- Possible valve issues (see valve section).

- Possible carbonator issues (see carb issue).

No soda water dispensing:

- Ensure there is an even ice bank and that ice is not touching the lines and is not frozen.

- Possible carb issues (see carb section).

- Possible valve issues (see valve section).

NOT dispensing syrup:

- Ensure ice bank is not frozen and has an even ice bank and ice is not touching lines.

- Possible BIB issues (see BIB section).

- Possible valve issues (see valves section).

NOTES

Chapter 12

Barguns

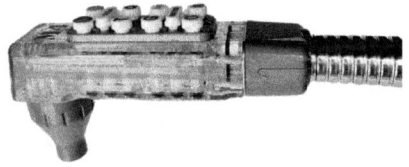

A bargun is normally found behind bars, hence the name bargun. Used to ensure the product is mixed correctly before dispensing into a cup or crafted beverage. Barguns are normally connected to an ice well using a cold-plate to ensure the product is dispensed at the right temp for a quality-tasting product.

Wonder bar Mark IV and S 2.5. Taprite Rattler 1 and 2. Taprite Magnum

Flat or foamy drinks or off tasting drinks:

- Low or no CO2 (see carbonator or C)2 pressures section).

- No ice in the ice bin chilling drinks.

- Improper ratio on bar gun.

- Possible ice has bridged up on the cold-plate not allowing lines to cool properly (below 41 degrees F).

- Ice bin drain clogged (ice bin holding water).

- Dirty or clogged Nozzle.

Bargun blowing air and syrup only:

- See carb section.

Leaking water or syrup from bar gun nozzle:

- Swollen or defective stem O-ring.

- Possible defective stem (check for pitting on stem).

- Broken or dirty butterfly retainer.

- Possible stem O-ring unseating causing stem to stick, use new updated O-rings (currently the blue ones).

Leaking water or syrup from bargun handle (Wonder Bar only):

- Possible cracked locking plug retainer plate.
- Possible bad locking plug or plug O-ring.
- Possible defective ferrule tube or ferrule tube cap.
- Possible cracked handle or loose screws on heel assembly.
- Loose or cracked nozzle or missing nozzle diffuser O-ring.

Leaking water or syrup from bargun handle (Taprite only):

- Possible cracked plunger retainer plate.
- Possible detective plunger retainer plate O-rings.
- Possible defective tubing and O-rings on heel assembly.
- Loose screws on heel assembly.
- Defective or missing nozzle seal.
- Possible crack in the handle.
- Loose or cracked nozzle.

After dispensing product, syrup continues to dispense:

- Swollen or defective stem O-ring or unseated stem O-ring.
- Possible detective stem (check for pitting on stem).

- Broken or dirty butterfly plate.

- Ensure the butterfly retainer is not over tight.

- Check for foreign debris where the stem and stem O-ring set.

- **DO NOT** soak barguns overnight in water or sanitizer. Only soak the nozzle in solution. Clean bargun handle with appropriate brush.

Syrup or water leaking from manifold:

- Possible defective adjusting screw tube retainer O-ring.

- Cracked module or flow control body, normally due to over tightened screws on flow control body or module.

- Possible pin hole in flow control (module).

- Possible leaking tubing or O-rings where bargun whip meets manifold.

- Possible cracked manifold or shut off.

NOT dispensing soda water or bargun blowing air:

- Remove the flow control and check for foreign debris or broken spring.

- See carb section for more info.

- Possible restriction on bargun tubing or handle.

- Shut off not in the open position.

NOT dispensing syrup:

- Remove the flow control and check for foreign debris or broken spring.

- Possible restriction in bargun tubing or handle.

- Shut-off not in the open position.

- See BIB section for more info.

Pineapple juice not dispensing:

- Normally caused from a clogged flow control.

- Ensure to use a juice meter stem flow control and not the spool with spring.

- Also ensure pineapple is not run through the cold-plate. By-pass cold pate and run line directly to the bargun manifold.

NOTES

Chapter 13

Automated beverage system

The automated beverage system is a beverage pouring system that reduces the need of crew members to pour drinks. Through a point-of-sales (POS) system, the order comes directly through to the ABS accurately pouring the correct size and flavor drink while delivering drinks on time with food orders.

ABS 1.0

Proper pressures for ABS 1.0 and ABS 2.0:

- Water booster pressure cut on at 70 PSI, off at 90 PSI.

- CO2 from bulk CO2 tank and carbonator tank 90 PSI.

- BIB regulator pressure 65 PSI.

- Bulk coke syrup CO2 pressure 60 PSI.

- Water regulator supplying carb motors set 55 PSI.

NOT dispensing syrup:

- Check for empty BIB.

- Check bag connector is screwed on properly.

- Ensure BIB line is not kinked.

- CO2 is on and set to 65 PSI and connected to BIB pump.

- Check multiplex water bath ice bank to ensure it's not frozen or ice bank is not touching the stainless steel coils.

- Make sure shut-off on syrup block is pushed down all the way in the open position.

- Remove the flow control and check for a broken spring or foreign debris in flow control spool and sleeve.

- Remove the plunger and check for a swollen tip or rusty plunger housing.

- Possible weak solenoid not pulling up the plunger.

- If there is no power to solenoid, it's possible the beverage interface board is defective.

No soda water flowing or low soda water flow:

- Check shut-off on soda water block is pushed down and in the 'open' position.

- Remove flow control and check for foreign debris or broken spring.

- Check plunger for a swollen tip or rusty plunger housing.

- Possible weak solenoid not pulling the plunger up.

- If there is no power to the solenoid, there is a possible defective beverage interface board.

- Possible high water pressure from the miltiplex, such as bad recirculating pump or no soda water coming from carb tank (see multiplex section for more info).

NOT dispensing ice:

- Ice bin is empty.

- Ice gate not opening, check for 60 PSI at the CO2 regulator near motion control board and ensure the CO2 shut off switch near the ice gate cylinder is in the 'on' position.

- Make sure there is a smooth action of the ice gate cylinder, and it's not binding up on the ice chute.

- Clump of ice blocking ice the chute opening.

- Ice gate sensor error due to a defective ice gate cylinder or ice gate sensor.

- Ice agitator motor not spinning allowing ice to fill the ice chute, or broken agitator blade or wheel.

Conveyor or turret continuously running at low speed:

- Replace the motion control board.

ABS intermittently reinitializes:

- Check all power and wire connections.

- Possible defective power supply board.

ABS 1.0 Errors

Clear cup jam:

- Normally caused because the full travel sensor on the side of the lift arm assembly did not detect a full up or full down travel during the timed up or down sequence. Check for a stuck or dirty lift arm assembly. Also check for broken or corroded wires to sensor.

- Possible faulty full travel sensor.

- Defective lift arm assembly.

Conveyor stalled:

- Normally caused because the index cup sensor is not reading the magnet on the bottom of conveyor cups. Check to make sure the cups are tight and secure on the belt, tighten the belt properly to 18 ¾ from center to center of shaft gears. Aalso make sure magnets are not missing on bottom of cups.

- Possible defective conveyor motor or gearbox.

- Possible defective motion control board.

- Possible defective conveyor motor or capacitor.

Turret stalled:

- Make sure the cup turret is spinning freely and not hitting the side of the unit.

- Make sure the turret encoder disc is clean, no rust, and is not bent.

- Possible defective turret sensor board.

- Bent or broken turret support shaft or bracket.

- Loose or broken disc hub or coupling.

- Possible defective turret motor or turret motor capacitor.

- Possible defective motion control board.

Ice gate error:

- The most common issue is a defective ice gate cylinder.

- Check to ensure the ice gate is moving freely and not binding up.

- Possible defective ice gate sensor.

- Ensure CO_2 pressure is set to 60 PSI.

Cup sold out when full:

- Check CO_2 pressure on ABS is set to 60 PSI.

- Ensure the grabber block is opening and closing properly.

- Make sure the grabber block switch (sensor) is adjusted properly. Using the bottom of a child size cup, close the arms clamp to the bottom of the cup. Slide the sensor from close to open then another 1/16 of an inch more then tighten down.

- Possible faulty or corroded wire connections from board to grabber block sensor.

- Ensure the grabber pads are not missing and are in good condition.

- Cup tube fingers bent and not releasing cups.

Wrap around error:

- Motion control, beverage interface board, or store sensor board are not communicating.

- Possible faulty or dirty wire harness connecting between the boards or one of the boards are defective.

Low CO2 alarm.

- Check CO2 on bulk tank to ensure it's set to 90 PSI.

- ABS regulator set to 60 PSI.

- Possible faulty CO2 low pressure switch.

Conveyor continuously spinning or not working:

- Normally caused from a bad conveyor motor or locked up gearbox.

- Possible defective motion control board or conveyor capacitor.

- See conveyor stalled error section.

Crushing cups on lift arm (grabber block arms):

- Normally caused from the index (cup sensor) not properly reading cups.

- See conveyor stalled error section for more info.

Off taste/Flat drinks:

- Check for proper CO2 pressure to carb tanks (90 PSI).

- Ensure there is an ice bank in the multiplex and recirculating motor and pump are functioning properly.

- Ensure there is ice in the ice bin and ABS has ice on the cold-plate.

- Improper ratio (see not dispensing soda water or not dispensing syrup section if unable to ratio).

- Missing or broke nozzle or diffuser.

Drink orders not coming through from the POS system:

- Check for missing pins on POS cable and no corrosion is present.

- Ensure the POS cable is plugged into the store sensor board and dispense a drink manually in automatic mode using the

ABS touchpad. If the ABS dispenses a drink, most likely it's a faulty POS cable or problem with POS system. If the ABS does not dispense a drink, most likely it's a problem with the ABS boards or a harness between boards not communicating.

Touchpad or displays not working:

- Possible defective touchpad or display.

- Possible defective harness connecting from the touchpad or display to the beverage interface board.

- Possible defective beverage interface board.

- No power to the beverage interface board.

Turret motor not working or continuously spinning:

- If the turret motor is continuously spinning, it's normally caused by a defective turret sensor board not reading the encoder disc.

- Possible defective turret motor,or defective motion control board.

- See turret motor stall error section for more info.

Lift arm problems/not grabbing cups:

- Enter test mode.

- Move lift arm up using test mode. If it does not move up,

check to ensure the CO2 pressure is set to 60 PSI. If correct, lower the ABS regulator CO2 pressure to 0 PSI and try to pull the lift arm up manually. If it does not move, replace the lift arm assembly. If it's sticking, clean the lift arm guide rods or replace the lift arm assembly.

- If it moves up, check the display to make sure it says up when the arm goes up, and down when the arm goes down, while moving freely. If the display is not reading properly when moving up or down, suspect broken or corroded wire connections from the motion control board to the lift arm reed switch (up and down lift arm sensor on side of arm) or a faulty lift arm sensor.

- Possible corroded wire connection on air flow control solenoid or defective air flow solenoid.

- Possible pinched air lines.

- Check cup sold out error section for more info or clear up jam error section.

NOT grabbing cups:

- Check to ensure the grabber block is opening and closing properly when operating. If opens or closes normal, then the last half of cycle is slow or lagging. Ensure CO2 regulator is set to 60 PSI. If correct, it's likely a defective grabber block or pinched umbilical CO2 line.

- Missing or worn grabber pads.

Under or over pouring drinks:

- Not enough ice in cups.

- Ensure proper ratio on drinks – 13oz soda, 12oz water.

- Correct portion setting to the cup's size.

- Ensure ice is filling the ice chute properly (no chunks of ice blocking the ice gate, ice agitator motor and the blade is spinning properly to fill the ice chute).

- Ice gate operating properly.

- Might need to adjust the top off delay on certain flavors.

- See ice gate sensor error section for more info.

Water leaking from random places (most common):

- Water leak from ice machine.

- Leak from flow controls, back block, or back block shut offs.

Grabbing multiple cups:

- Missing, broke, or bent cup tube finger assembly.

- Cups packed in too tight and the customer not fanning (separating) cups when refilling cup tube.

ABS 2.0

Proper pressures for ABS 1.0 and ABS 2.0:

- Water booster pressure cut on at 70 PSI, off at 90 PSI.

- CO_2 from bulk CO_2 tank and carbonator tank at 90 PSI.

- BIB regulator pressure at 65 PSI.

- Bulk coke syrup CO_2 pressure at 60 PSI.

- Water regulator supplying carb motors set at 55 PSI.

Soda water not dispensing:

- Ensure the backroom water and CO_2 pressure are correct.

- Check the recirculation pump to ensure it's operating correctly. If it's bad, it could be causing pressure build up, causing the soda water solenoid armature tips to fail and not allow them to open up correctly to let soda water flow through.

- Ensure the valve is on the back block correctly and the shut-offs are in the open position.

- Remove the flow control and check for foreign debris or a broken spring.

- Check the plunger for a swollen tip or rusty plunger housing.

- Possible weak solenoid not pulling up the plunger.

- If you've replaced the solenoid assembly and it's still not activating, check for a possible faulty wire harness or defective MFV board.

- If you find yourself replacing the same solenoid over the course of a few weeks or couple months, suspect a defective wire harness to the solenoids.

- If there is no water or soda water, see multiplex section for more information.

NOT dispensing ice:

- The ice bin is empty.

- If the ice gate is not opening, ensure the main ABS regulator is set to 60 PSI (controlled by ice gate solenoid 35 PSI).

- Possible defective ice gate cylinder.

- Clump of ice blocking the ice gate opening.

- Ensure the ice chute cover is properly attached and is not missing the magnet.

- Possible defective ice agitator motor not spinning allowing ice to fill ice chute.

- Possible broken agitator blade or wheel.

NOT dispensing syrup:

- Check for empty BIB.

- Ensure the bag connectors are screwed on properly.

- Ensure the BIB line is not kinked.

- CO_2 is on and set to 65 PSI and connected to the bottom of pump. 60 PSI on bulk Coke syrup tank.

- Check the water bath on the multiplex to ensure the ice bank is not touching the stainless steel coils.

- Make sure the shut-off on the syrup back block is in the on position.

- Remove the flow control and check for a broken spring or foreign debris in the flow control.

- Remove the syrup solenoid and check for a swollen plunger tip or a rusty plunger housing.

- Possible weak solenoid not pulling up the plunger.

- If you've replaced the solenoid assembly and it's still not activating, it could possibly be a defective wire harness or a defective MFV board.

Errors

Remove last cup from staging area:

- Make sure the cup carousel is on properly (thumb screws tightened down) and **NO** lose cups on the belt.

- Ensure there is no ice or foreign objects in the carousel cups.

- Make sure the last cup sensor is clean.

- Last cup sensor may need recalibrated.

- Possible faulty last cup sensor.

Carousel motor stall:

- Ensure there are no cups, ice, lids or foreign objects blocking carousel from moving.

- Carousel is not installed properly.

- Dirty or sticky conveyor belt.

- In auto mode with carousel not installed.
- Possible faulty index sensor.
- Possible faulty carousel motor.
- Possible faulty motion control board.

Cup failed to dispense from tube/or not grabbing cups:

- Missing or worn gripper pads.
- Damaged cup tube fingers not releasing cups.
- Ensure CO_2 pressure from the back room is set to 90 PSI and ABS is set between 54-60 PSI.
- Possible faulty proximity sensor on picker assembly.
- Possible faulty picker assembly.

Push in ice chute cover or lid:

- Ensure the ice chute cover is attached properly, and the magnet is not missing.
- Ensure the manual ice fill lid is closed properly.
- Possible faulty ice fill lid switch.

CO_2 low or sold out:

- Ensure supply CO_2 or air is above 80 PSI.

- Possible faulty CO2 sold out sensor.

Turret motor time out:

- Ensure the turret assembly is installed correctly and the pin is not damaged or broken.
- Make sure the encoder disc is clean, no rust, and not bent.
- Possible defective encoder board.
- Check for bent or broken turret shaft or bracket.
- Check for a loose coupling on the turret motor shaft.
- Check for loose screws on the turret motor.
- Possible defective turret motor.
- Possible defective motion control board.

Grabbing multiple cups:

- Missing or bent cup tube finger assembly.
- Cups are packed in too tight and not fanning the cups when refilling cup tube.

Turret door not opening:

- Ensure the turret door gasket on the left side is not missing.
- Possible faulty turret door switch (check for water leaking on the switch).

- Possible defective MFV board.

Drinks under or over filling:

- Check carb and water flow is set to 12oz.
- Check ice portion amount to ensure it's set to the proper cup sizes.
- Ensure the ice chute is filling properly before dropping ice into the cup.
- Ratio valve.
- Ensure the top off delay is set on flavors needed.

The syrup carries over to another drink:

- Diffuser (gasket) not installed correctly.
- Missing or dirty diffuser or nozzle assembly.

POS issue:

- Verify the cat 5 cable is connected and working. Verify the connection status in the NP6 menu. Check for operational status, make sure it's showing up. If it is, it's good. If showing down, there is possibly a bad connection on machine, faulty cable, or POS system issue.
- Invalid POS order – POS system parameters are not set to a valid valve or to a brand not supported.

Unit continuously restarting:

- Ensure the ice chute manual fill lid is closed and properly latched.

- Ensure the ice chute cover is attached properly.

- Possible ABS software corrupted on needs updated.

Display touchscreen issue:

- Reboot ABS. Ensure 30 seconds between power off and power on.

- **Blue recovery screen:** Ensure when powered off you wait at least 30 seconds before powering the ABS back on.

- Possible corrupted software will need to be deleted and the updated software installed.

Right or left screen white (reboot the ABS):

- Using a keyboard plugged into the USB port on the back of the screen, press the windows and P key simultaneously. Select the extend option tab and press enter to activate the other screen. If this did not fix the issue, replace the screen.

Duplicate screens or one screen on:

- Reboot the ABS access windows by swiping right on the right side of the left screen or plug a keyboard on the back of the screen. Go to start>control panel>display>display settings, then select the drop down menu on multiple displays and select extend multiple displays and hit apply, then keep changes. If it doesn't work, there's possibly a bad display.

Cups on the conveyer are being crushed by the grabber arms:

- Ensure the carousel is properly installed and clean.

- Ensure the last cup sensor is clean, calibrated and not displaying error messages.

- If the last cup sensor error is showing up on the display and is crushing cups, it could be a faulty or dirty last cup sensor.

- Possible faulty index sensor (cup sensor).

Off taste or flat drinks:

- Check for proper CO_2 pressure to the carbonator tanks (90 PSI).

- Ensure the multiplex has a good ice bank and the recirculating pump and motor are functioning properly.

- Ensure the ice bin is full and ABS has ice on the cold-plate.

- Missing or dirty diffuser, diffuser seal, or nozzle assembly.

- Improper ratio (see not dispensing soda water or not dispensing syrup section if unable to ratio).

NOTES

NOTES

Chapter 14
Multiplex Chiller

A multiplex is used to pre-chill the product and water before it reaches the beverage equipment. It eliminates the need for cold-plates or, when used in combination with a cold plate, will reduce ice consumption and ensure the product is delivered at the optimal temperature.

No soda flow or low soda flow/no water flow:

- Check CO2 pressure at bulk tank set to 90 PSI and shut off is in the 'on' position:

- CO2 switch over valve is turned to bulk tank and shut-off valve on multiplex supplying CO2 to the carb tanks is in the 'open' position.

- Check ice bank in the water bath and ensure it is not touching the stainless steel lines.

- Ensure there is a good water supply, good water filters, and that the water regulators on the side of the multiplex that supply water to the carb tank is set to 55 PSI, and that the water booster is set to come on at 70 PSI and cut off at 90 PSI.

- Check for water flow at incoming water line at carb pump (brass pump).

- Possible defective recirculating pump (stainless pump) causing build up of pressure.

Carb pump and motor issues (brass pump):

- If the motor is not turning on, check that the on/off switch is on and supplying power to the motor. If not, then unplug the carb probe wires on the board. If it turns on, then it could be faulty carb wires or defective carb probes. If it does not come on, it could be a defective board. If it has a liquid level control board, remove the green ground wire to make the motor turn on temporarily.

- Possible faulty 4 PSI water safety switch killing power to all motors.

- **Motor not turning on and getting hot** – bad or locked up carb pump or motor. Check for correct voltage.

- **Motor turning on and getting hot (not filling tank).**

- No water to the pump, bad or locked up pump or motor.

- Bad backflow preventer (check valve) causing back pressure, not allowing water to fill the carb tank.

Carbonator tank relief valve blowing:

- Check carb tank probe wires to ensure green ground wire is secured to the tank.

- Possible defective ERC board or liquid level control board for liquid level control board. Verify by creating a 3-wire jumper with spade connectors on one end and that all three wires are tied together at the other end. Remove probe wires from board (Hi-Low-G) and connect a 3-wire jumper to Hi-Low-G on the liquid level control board. Turn power back on. If it continues to run, replace the board. If it does not run, suspect faulty carb probe wires, connections, or defective carb probes.

The water bath is frozen:

- Ensure the water bath agitator is spinning and agitating water.

- Possible defective ice bank control causing the compressor to continually run.

- Possible defective ice bank control probe (sensor) or probe (sensor) not in the correct location. Ensure it's secured properly.

Compressor not turning on and running:

- Power switch not turned to the on position.

- Possible defective ice bank control or ice bank control probe sensor.

- Possible defective board.

- Possible TDS level of water below 100 PPM not allowing electrical conductivity through the water. If suspected, drain water bath and refill with fresh water.

- Possible compressor or component issues.

Uneven ice bank:

- Usually caused by low freon or restriction in the refrigeration system.

- Ice bank control sensor not in proper location or secured properly.

- Unit was partially thawed then turned back on. Ice bank must be completely thawed if the ice bank is uneven or melted before returning to normal operation.

Water lines blowing off or recirculation pump:

- If the water lines blow off the pump and the clamp is still on the line, suspect a faulty recirculation pump causing the pump lines to heat up, blowing the line off the pump. Replace recirculation pump.

Water or syrup lines bursted or hole in lines:

- Replace the whole piece of tubing, do not try and patch. Beverage line has been compromised, usually due to being pinched off, line old, or cut prior with dull tubing cutters. Ensure tubing cutter blade is changed frequently.

Error Codes

E1 low water supply pressure drops below 5 PSI for 5 seconds:

- Ensure the water booster works properly, cycling on at 70 PSI and off at 90 PSI (see water booster section).

- Ensure the water filters are good and filtered water pressure gauge on the multiplex is reading 55 PSI.

- Possible defective water pressure switch or transducer.

- Possible defective ERC board (less common).

E2 low CO2 pressure:

- The CO2 pressure drops below 10 PSI for 5 seconds.

- Ensure correct CO2 pressure to the unit is 90 PSI.

- Possible defective CO2 pressure switch or transducer.

- Possible defective ERC board (less common).

E3 low water level:

- Caused when the water bath level drops below the level probe.

- If water is above probe possible defective probe.

- Possible defective ERC board.

- Ensure the probe is secured in the correct location.

E4 high water bath temperature:

- Caused by water bath above 45 degrees.

- Check to ensure the ice bank and water agitator are working properly.

- Possible defective water bath thermistor (temp probe).

- Possible detective ERC board (less common).

- Ensure probe is secured in correct the location.

E5 high water supply pressure:

- Caused by water pressure above 75 PSI.

- Possible defective high water pressure regulator, ensure it's set at 55 PSI.

E6 high refrigeration temperature:

- Caused by liquid side temperature above 200 degrees.

- Verify with a thermometer. If below 200 degrees, suspect a defective liquid line thermistor or defective ERC board. If above 200 degrees, ensure the condenser is clean and operating properly.

- Possible defective hot gas bypass.

- Possible refrigeration issues.

E7 high ice bank size:

- Normally caused by ice on the middle pin of ice bank probe.

- Verify ice is on the middle pin. If so, suspect a defective ice bank probe or ERC board. Also ensure the ice bank is even. **IF NOT** troubleshoot refrigeration system.

E8/E9 by carbonator motor running continuously for 7 minutes:

- Caused by long run time on carb A or carb B.

- Ensure good water pressure to the carb pump.

- Possible detective carbonator pump or motor.

- Check the carb probe harness to ensure green ground wire is secured to the tank. Also ensure harness connections are not loose or broken wires in the harness.

- Possible defective backflow preventer or check valve.

- Check lines and valves to ensure there are no soda water leaks.

- Possible defective ERC board.

Display reading *shorted transducer*:

- Check for broken wires on the thermistors, replace the defective thermistor (located on carb recirculating lines).

NOTES

Chapter 15
Juice Dispenser

A juice dispenser is used to dispense products such as orange juice and apple juice and is normally found in restaurants or hotels that serve breakfast. It has a self contained refrigeration unit to chill product to proper temperature as well as assuring the product is mixing properly to give you the correct ratio of concentrate and water to ensure a quality drink.

Lancer MMJ 2 and MMJ 4 Units

Low water pressure error:

- Ensure proper water supply to unit is a minimum of 40 PSI.

- Possible defective water valve assembly or defective concave flow washer.

Leaking syrup from nozzle or not priming:

- Possible dirty or detective nozzle assembly.

- Possible loose connection or defective O-rings on check valve connection on product container. Verify tubing connections on the check valve and that the pump housing is tight and secure.

- Possible loose pump housing cover or defective housing cover O-ring.

- Check and ensure the syrup delivery tubes on the package platform base are not cracked and the O-rings are not missing or defective.

Not priming:

- Ensure product is thawed properly (thaw in cooler for 48-72 hours prior to using).

- Ensure there are no air or syrup leaks in syrup delivery system.

- Possible dry or defective pump impeller.

- Possible defective pump, a.k.a. stepper motor (less common).

- Loose wire connection on pump or board.

- Possible defective board (less common).

No power to unit:

- Ensure there is correct power on the outlet.

- Ensure the breaker is not tripped on the machine.

- Ensure the power supply cord on the machine is plugged in properly.

- Possible defective PC board.

- Possible defective key switch.

Door display of buttons not working:

- Ensure the door board is not loose and is secured properly.

- Possible defective door board.

- Possible defective door board wire harness from the PC board to the door board.

- Ensure key switch is in the on position.

Warm product dispense:

- Ensure the cabinet fan is working properly.

- Ensure the door is closed.

- Possible refrigeration deck issues not cooling properly.

The product has an off taste:

- Improper ratio.

- Out of date product. Ensure the correct product being dispensed is the product displayed on the LED display.

Ratio settings:

- To check ratio, you need a 500 mL graduated cylinder.

- Turn key switch to flush position.

- Press the two outside buttons on the door. * and # symbol to enter ratio menu.

- Follow directions on the display.

- Dispense water only into 500 mL cylinder (it should read 450 mL). Pour out and dispense again. Finished product will dispense. It should match the water dispensed at 450 mL. If the level is above (example 5 mL) enter + 5 mL. If it's below 5 mL, enter -5 mL. When done, turn the key switch to the on position. It is now ready to use.

NOTES

Chapter 16
Vending Machine

A vending machine is an automated dispensing machine with a self contained refrigeration unit that ensures products stay at a preferred temperature around 37 degrees. Normally accepts payment with coins, cash, or credit cards to dispense products.

Crane Merchandising systems (Dixie Narco)

Takes money but won't vend:

- Ensure product is not jammed and spacers are set correctly.

- During test vend, if you hear vend motor activate for a split second, suspect a defective vend motor switch. Also check to see if the vend motor switch arm is centered with the cam opening on the vend motor. If the switch lever is off center, replace the switch.

- During the a test vend, if the motor is activating but the rotor cup is not rotating, releasing drinks. Suspect a broken vend motor linkage that connects motor to rotor cup. Also check for drink jam.

- **If it vends no product then vends two the next time,** suspect a possible twisted rotor cup or oscillator. Ensure the proper shims are in place (can or bottle). Double columns have a can or bottle shim that must be in place. Also for E models, the single columns will need a rod and spring for cans. Normally fits in the center hole location in the rotor cup.

    - Ensure vend motor cam is set to the proper position. To desired depth **(2 deep)**, **(3 deep)**, **(4 deep)**, etc.

    - Possible defective vend motor switch.

Taking money but the column is empty (motor still rotating):

- Possible defective sold out switch.

- Check wire connections on sold out switch.

- Ensure the sold out paddle is not bent and is engaging the sold out switch when the column is empty.

Machine reads out of service:

- Possible defective vend motor switch. Was free vending then control board took it out of service.

- Check for a blown fuse on the board. Possible jammed column caused fuse to blow.

- Possible defective control board.

Flavor selection button not working:

- Possible defective selection switch.

- Check selection switch wiring.

- Possible blown fuse on board or defective control board.

Product freezing up:

- Ensure the temperature probe is in the correct location.

- Temp setting not at max setting.

- Possible defective temperature controller.

TECH TIP!! Smack temp control with a piece of wood or end of a screwdriver. If it shuts off, replace temp control.

The product is hot:

- Compressor running and all fans working, suspect low freon or restriction in refrigeration system.

- Ensure the evaporator fan motor is working and the evaporator is not frozen over.

- If frozen, check to ensure outside air is not getting into the machine. Ensure the door is closing properly, and that the drink port door is not broken. The door should be closing properly and the door seal needs to be sealing good. If the door and seal are fine, but it's still frozen, suspect faulty temp control. Ensure the machine is level.

- If frozen just across the top or half way down the evaporator, suspect the machine is low on freon or there is a restriction in the system.

- Ensure the drain tube is not clogged.

- If the product is hot and the compressor is not turning on, ensure there is correct power to the machine and the compressor deck is plugged in.

- Possible defective temp control. **TECH TIP!!** If off, smack the end of a screwdriver or piece of wood on the temp control. If it comes on, replace temp control.

- Possible defective temp sensor or control board.

- Possible defective fan or compressor replays.

Insert change but no credit reading on display:

- Ensure the display is working properly.

- Check for jam in coin chute.

- Possible jam in coin mech.

- Possible defective coin mech.

For space to sales or programming, see https;//rc.cranems.com

Free vending or motor continuously spinning:

- Normally a defective vend motor switch.

- Ensure all the wire connections to the vend motor switch and control board are not broken and secure.

- Possible blown fuse on the control board.

- Check to ensure the vend motor brake is moving freely (not sticking) and brake is not broke or missing.

Vending wrong product:

- Make sure the product is loaded in the correct columns.

- Need to set space to sales in the control board menu. Check to ensure the columns are programmed to the correct selection buttons.

NOT accepting dollar bills:

- Ensure there is change in the coin mech. Most machines need at least a roll of nickels in the coin tubes to accept dollars.

- Ensure there is power to the coin mech and that the coin mech is working correctly and is not jammed.

- Ensure belts on the validator are not torn or broken.

- Clean validator sensors and ensure the bill path is not obstructed or dirty.

- Possible defective bill validator.

Dollar bill goes in half way then returns bill:

- Ensure prizm on bottom of the bill box is flush with the box and is not sticking out.

- Possible foreign debris jammed in validator.

- Clean validator sensors.

- Ensure the door switch is working properly and that the switch is engaged.

- Possible short in wiring or loose connections.

Display reading homing:

- Check for product jam in the column.

- Possible detective vend switch on the motor.

- Check to ensure the rotor cup is rotating without hitting anything. Possible back spacer sitting to low hitting rotor or oscillator.

Vending wrong product:

- Ensure columns are loaded correctly.

- Check space-to-sales settings (more than one column may be programmed to one selection).

- Possible miswired selection button.

Price reading $99.99 or losing memory:

- Replace battery on board.

Coins not falling into coin mech or building on top of coin mech:

- Ensure the coin mech mounting screws are tightened securely.

- Ensure the coin chute is properly aligned and not damaged.

- Ensure the coin deflector on coin chute is not missing and in the proper position (at end of coin chute near coin mech).

Display reading sold out but the machine is full:

- Suspect a faulty door switch.

Sales numbers not showing on display when the door is open:

- Ensure the configuration setting is turned on to display totals.

- Possible defective door switch.

NOT accepting coins:

- Possible jammed coin mech, check coin acceptor and coin dispense arms.

- Dirty sensors on coin acceptor.

- Coin mech must have at least a roll of nickels in the coin mech tubes.

- Ensure the door switch is working properly and the door switch is engaged.

- Check for a coin chute jam and that the coin mech is aligned properly.

- Possible short in the wiring or loose wire connection.

- Possible defective coin mech.

- Possible defective control board.

Coins falling through to the coin return cup:

- Stuck coin return button on machine or coin return lever on coin mech.

- Jam in change acceptor.

- Defective or dirty coin mech.

- No power to the coin mech.

Coins falling into wrong coin tubes:

- Check for jam in coin mech.

- Coin mech not programed correctly.

- Defective coin mech.

Incorrect change:

- Coin mech or cassette is not programed correctly.

- Dirty or sticky coins are not dispensing.

- Broken or defective coin mech dispensing arms.

Can't read display or no power to display:

- Check for loose or corroded wire connections to the display.

- Possible defective display.

- Possible defective control board.

Dixie DN 3800 - DN 5800

- **Glass Front Vendor**

Bev max 4 3800-5800-bermax refresh 4 DN5800-414c, see https://re.cranems.com for full service and parts manuals.

Process to ensure X, Y, and cup assembly home switches are in the home position:

- Press the **program button** on the control board and ensure the display reads **Error codes**, then enter the factory password, **15151**. The display should read **Bevmax setup.** Press the number 2 key to scroll till the display reads **Position test**. Pull the left door switch out and press the **enter key number 4.**

Press the F key to ensure the machine is in the full home position. Next look at the LED lights on the control board. You should see a **RED LED** light (cup assembly picker home switch), **AMBER LED** light (X home switch at top left side of Y motor assembly) and a **GREEN LED** light (Y home switch at bottom of product cup). If any of these lights are not lit up on the board, troubleshoot the home switch that is not showing home on the control board.

Product not vending into cup assembly:

- Check to ensure the tray slide is clean and that the pusher spring is not broken. If the product is not sliding correctly or dispensing into cup assembly at an angle, clean and spray with food grade silicone. If problem persists, replace tray slide assembly.

- Ensure the gate is not sticking or that it is not broken.

- Ensure the plunger and gearbox are not broken and are functioning correctly.

Product cup cycled but product did not fully dispense:

- Ensure the gate is not sticking or broke.

- Check to ensure the product shelf tray is properly secured to tray supports.

If the cup assembly plunger is hitting the shelf during dispense:

- Ensure the harness and x motor connections are secure.

- Check to ensure the belt is not slipping during test vend.

- May need to adjust the shelf offset in the control board settings. Ensure cup assembly plunger is contacting shelf dispense plunger in between the two lines on shelf plunger approximately ¼ from the top of shelf dispense plunger.

LED Display not working.

- If the display is out but lights on the machine are working. It could be caused by electrical interference.

- Separate the LED display harness wire to ensure it's not contacting the other wires near the display.

- Possible defective LED display.

- Possible faulty display harness.

Picker or vend mechanism error:

- Normally caused from the product cup assembly.

- Ensure the product cup assembly plunger is cycling properly and not sticking due to syrup buildup.

- Ensure bottles are not blocking the elevator arm from moving freely.

- If the cup assembly plunger is stuck in the out position, you can reset the plunger. To **reset procedure**, press mode button on control board, press 15151 on the touchpad to enter programing. Press 4, the press 2, until you see position test and the press 4 to pull out the left door switch. Press 0 and the plunger should go back in. Press F to home cup if not already at home, test vend, and vend with money. Should be fixed. If the problem persists, replace cup assembly.

- Ensure the cup assembly is going to the home position.

- Possible defective X or Y home switches. Verify in test mode with the top door switch pressed in. Ensure product cup assembly is in the home position. Check the LED lights on the control board. The X home (top left switch) will light up an amber color. The Y home (bottom left switch) will light up a green color if in the home position.

Elevator will not move vertically or horizontally:

- Ensure no product is jammed or blocking elevator from moving freely.

- Check to ensure the elevator rollers are not worn out or broken.

- Ensure the product cup assembly home switch and plunger are not stuck out.

- Check to ensure the door switches are working properly and making contact when the door is closed.

- Possible defective X or Y vend motor or harness.

- Possible defective X, Y board.

- Possible defective control board.

Product cup assembly slams against right side or misses hook when trying to vend product:

- You may need to adjust the hook offset in the control board settings.

Product vends into port assembly but doesn't open (reads sold out):

- Possible defective vend sensor or loose or broken wire connections to the port vend sensor.

Port assembly problems:

- If the port door does not open fully, check to ensure wires are not blocking the port door from opening properly. Ensure the port door is closed and not jammed on port assembly.

- Port assembly stays fully opened or bounces between open and closed. Check to ensure nothings blocking it from moving freely.

- Check for broken port motor cam (black piece).

- Possible defective port assembly board (check for broken or missing switches).

Evaporator ice build up from bottom causing a water leak:

- Check to ensure there is no outside air getting inside the machine. Check panels around the evaporator and wire holes for possible air entries into the cabinet. All gaps or holes should be filled with Permagum putty.

- Ensure the vender door seal is sealing properly.

- Possible clogged evaporator drain line to drain pan.

- Ensure the vender is level and not leaning forward.

- Possible defective evaporator fan motor.

- Possible refrigeration issues. Also ensure the back of the machine is a minimum of four inches from the wall and the condenser is clean with good airflow.

Royal GIll 3D vis plus

Royal 550, 600, 670, 804 machines

Takes money but won't vend:

- Possible jam in bill validator, coin mech, or coin chute.

- Possible defective chute sensor (drop sensor).

- Chute sensor not set correctly. Recommend starting position. Turn screw adjustment on the board clockwise until the light on the board turns on. Then turn the adjustment screw counter clockwise ½ to 2 full turns. Then adjust accordingly.

- Possible defective coin mech or validator.

- Check to ensure there is no short in the wiring.

- Possible defective control board.

Free vending:

- If it drops one, then drops another one seconds later, suspect the chute sensor is not set correctly or there is a defective chute sensor, also ensure the ground wire is properly grounded on the control board.

- Possible defective control board not allowing the chute sensor to adjust properly.

- If it drops multiple products at one time, suspect a defective or worn release lever and pivot ends.

- Check for missing or broken release lever spring.

- Possible product stop not set correctly to the correct product size.

- Check the control board depth settings for columns (1 or 2 deep).

Machine reads out of order:

- Ensure the vend chain assembly is not missing magnets on the chain.
- Vend chain is not broken or jammed.
- Possible defective home sensor or wiring.
- Possible defective vend motor or wiring.
- Possible defective control board.
- Ensure the vend chain is moving freely and aligned on the pivots.
- No power to the coin mech.
- The machine is empty (no product).
- Ensure the idler sprocket and springs are properly aligned and are not missing.

Price and space to sales resetting to default (losing memory).

- Replace the battery on the control board.
- Possible defective control board.

Vend chain continuously spinning (does not find home).

- Check for missing magnets on vend chain.

- Possible defective home sensor or wiring.

- Ensure the control board is grounded.

- Possible defective control board.

Vend chain stops at column but doesn't reverse to vend product:

- Suspect a defective vend motor or wiring.

- Possible defective control board.

Product jamming in column:

- Ensure the product stop is set to the correct product size.

- Soft or damaged product.

- Back or front spacers are not set correctly.

- Missing or broken release lever spring.

- Check for a broken pivot end or pivot pawl.

- Possible sticky or rusty pivot assembly rod not allowing the pivots to spin freely.

Adjust chute sensor (drop sensor).

- Turn screw adjustment on the control board clockwise till a red light on the board comes on, then turn the adjustment screw counter clockwise 1 ½ to 2 full turns. Then adjust accordingly.

- Ensure the sensor only comes on when the product hits the chute. Use end column when testing.

RVV 500 Vision Vendor (Royal glass front machine)

See https://royalvendors.com or full service and parts manuals.

Product cup assembly not finding home:

- Ensure the home sensor magnet bracket is not broken and the magnet is not missing. It should be facing out and flush with the front edge of the bottom shelf.

- Ensure the elevator assembly is level with the bottom door. If not, hold the higher side and push up on the lower side to level.

- Possible defective hall effect sensor, cup logic board, or DMC board.

- Check voltage on cup logic board P4 (red and black wire), it should be 5VDC. If no voltage is found, check voltage on P1 (green and black wires). If 5VDC is found, replace the cup board. If no voltage is found, check position P3 on the DMC board. If voltage is found, replace the harness from the DMC board to the cup board. If voltage 5VDC not found, replace the DMC board.

Product cup performs delivery test but stops short or slams against the left wall:

- Ensure the port slide door is engaging the port door switch. Check for missing or defective port door springs.

- Possible defective port door switch or switch wiring.

- May need to recalibrate the cup to find the home position. Ensure magnet is not missing and magnet bracket is flush with bottom shelf. With the door open, press and hold the 2 door switches. The cup assembly will go from left to right to recenter itself. After finished, close the door and test with money.

Cup assembly not opening sliding port door:

- Check to ensure the cup trip arm or trip bracket are not missing.

- If it's barely missing the hook trip arm bracket, you can bend the trip arm on the cup assembly to engage the bracket. If it's too far, you may need to adjust the calibration on the X port.

Product cup not finding home and moving up and down about 6 inches before going out of service:

- Ensure the elevator arm is level and engaging the vertical home switch.

- Check to ensure the vertical home switch wires are not broke or corroded.

- Possible defective vertical home switch.

- Possible defective DMC board.

Product cup does not move up or down:

- Check wire connection on Y motor.

- Possible defective Y motor.

- Possible defective wire harness to Y motor.

- Possible defective DMC board.

Product cup performs delivery test but elevator assembly does not move (just noise):

- Check to ensure X or Y belts and pulleys are not broke, loose, and not slipping.

- Possible defective X or Y motor.

Product cup not pulling product into cup:

- Ensure the product shelves are seated properly in the shelf rails.

- Ensure the shelf is straight and does not have a bow in it.

- Ensure the machine is level and the door is closed properly.

- Ensure the elevator and cup assembly are moving freely.

- Check to ensure the X magnet is not missing (located behind price stickers on odd columns).

- Possible broken or defective product retainers.

- Possible defective cup plunger or shelf worm gear were plunger contacts.

Vender display remove product:

- Ensure the sliding port door is clinging properly and engaging the switch.

- Ensure the port door bin is closed properly and moving freely.

- Ensure the port door bin is empty and free of debris.

- Possible defective or dirty emitter (lower) or detector (upper) boards.

- Check for 5VDC on DMC and VMC boards. DMC P4 on the black and brown wires. VMC P11 on the red an black wires. If no voltage is found, replace the board with no power.

Vendo V21 series Vmax 521-V621-V721-V821 Vending machines

Take money won't vend:

- Possible defective chute censor. Check the chute sensor LED. If on continuously, replace vend sensor.

- Possible defective control board. Unplug sensors from the control board. If the light stays on, replace the control board.

- Ensure the product is not jammed and the spacers are set correctly.

- Possible jam in the coin chute or coin mech.

- Possible jam in the bill validator.

Free vending:

- Possible defective chute sensors.

- Make sure the chute sensors are not unplugged from the connection underneath the drink chute.

- Ensure the column depth setting is set to the correct position for the product.

- Possible defective vend motor.

The machine is reading sold out:

- Check if the vend sensor is unplugged.

- Possible defective chute sensor.

- Check for product jam in column.

- Possible defective control board.

Display not working:

- Possible defective display or wire harness to display.

- Possible defective control board.

The board is losing memory or is resetting to a default price or space to sales:

- Replace the battery on the board.

- Possible defective control board.

Scaling factor error:

- Defective coin mech or coin mech harness.

- Possible defective bill validator or validator harness.

See https://vendnetusa.com for more info or trouble shooting

NOTES

NOTES

NOTES

REFERENCES

"Carbinators." Lancer Worldwide: Soda Fountain Dispensers. Last modified August 1, 2024. https://www.lancerworldwide.com/

"Flomatic." Multiplex Beverage - Home. Last modified 2024. https://www.multiplexbeverage.com/.

"Lancer 3.0 and 4.5." Lancer Worldwide. Last modified August 8, 2024. https://lancerbeverage.com/.

ManualsLib. "Cornelius ABS unit 1.0 and 2.0." ManualsLib - Makes it easy to find manuals online!. Last modified 2024. https://www.manualslib.com.

Pentair. "Bag-in-Box Syrup Pumps-Flojet N5100." Pentair | Move, Improve and Enjoy Water. Last modified 2024. https://pentair.com.

"Royal Vending Machines." Royal Vendors, Inc. – Global Leader in Refrigerated Beverage Vending Machines – Made In America. Last modified 2024. https://www.royalvendors.com/

REFERENCES

"Taprite and McCann's large reserve low profile." A Preferred Supplier for the Soda and Beer Industries. Last modified 2024. https://www.taprite.com

"Valves-Cornelius FFV-UF-1-SFV-1-Prisim." Cornelius USA. Last modified July 6, 2023. https://www.cornelius.com/.

"Vending Machines." CMS. Accessed August 19, 2024. https://rc.cranems.com/.

"VENDO V21 USER MANUAL Pdf Download." ManualsLib. Last modified September 13, 2017. https://www.manualslib.com/manual/1284040/Vendo-V21.html.

www.ingramcontent.com/pod-product-compliance
Lightning Source LLC
LaVergne TN
LVHW010334070526
838199LV00065B/5743